MW01518667

The Manifesto of Entrepreneurial Democracies

Alexandre Raab

Sagesse Editions
A division of SIRDAN PUBLISHING
Montreal, Quebec

**THE MANIFESTO OF ENTREPRENEURIAL
DEMOCRACIES**

CANADIAN CATALOGUING IN PUBLICATION DATA

Raab, Alexandre, 1924-

The Manifesto of Entrepreneurial Democracies

ISBN 0-921240-02-3 (bound)   0-921240-00-7 (pbk.)

1. Democracy.   2. Entrepreneurship   I. Title

JC423.R22 1989   321.8   C90-095356-2

First published in 1988 by
> **Sagessse Editions**
> Division of Sirdan Publishing
> P.O. Box 217
> Station T.M.R.
> Montreal, Quebec
> CANADA H3P 3B9

Printed and bound in Canada

DEDICATION

I dedicate this book to the memory of my parents,

SIMON AND SERENA RAAB,

for giving me the gift of life,

for engraving in my soul the respect for the dignity of man,

compassion toward the weak and feeble,

the uncompromising love of freedom

and the indomitable courage to speak up and fight for it.

You can rejoice in our victory.

Your detractors could never bring down your

sons and daughters to their level of bestiality.

ACKNOWLEDGEMENTS

Many thanks to my editor, Diana Marquise for her professional perseverance to be forceful, but never condescending. Anyone who has ever tried to tell a stubborn old farmer what to do will appreciate the challenge she faced to transfer my manuscript into an orderly book.

Alexandre Raab
Goodwood, Ontario

Contents

Preface

All of us who are the fortunate citizens of any of the entrepreneurial democracies, from Western Europe to Japan to North America, enjoy a standard of living and individual freedom unique in the history of man.

Because prosperity and freedom are such a natural condition of our existence, we tend to accept them as if they are provided by nature herself. For those of us born to abundance and freedom, it is difficult to comprehend the sacrifices paid by generations and generations to achieve this benign state of existence.

Freedom is like oxygen in the air. It is intangible, and invisible to the naked eye. We understand its existence only when we are exposed to an environment lacking it. This is an experience which is difficult for the intellect to perceive, but when experienced, it is easy to comprehend.

Today, this great fortune is threatened, as always, by hostile forces. Because most living members of our fortunate societies were born in freedom, the appreciation of its value diminishes year by year. Our desire and commitment to defend it is eroding.

This book is an attempt to redefine the substance of the social and economic system that provides us with this abundance of wealth and freedom, and to demonstrate that the alternatives available to us will inevitably bring about the loss of individual freedom and the lowering of our living standards.

I am a horticulturist by vocation and profession and very good at it, if I may say so. I attribute my success to the fact that I learned early in my 50 years of professional life that the power of observation is the most important guideline in practice when one is producing living things. Plants, like all living things, are imprinted by their biology, and success in raising them depends upon the skill to cater to their biological needs under local environmental conditions and the myriad vagaries of the weather.

An early experience left with me an everlasting lesson. About 30 years ago I purchased a 400-acre farm which included springs, a stream, ponds and marshlands with natural brook trout, a remnant of a forest of natural maple and other hardwoods, plus acres of planted red pines and spruce. I was anxious to retain this unique treasure and beauty of nature, so I consulted the various experts in the fishery and forestry departments.

First, the fishery expert told me I was mistaken, there could be no natural trout reproducing in ponds of this type. This statement inspired me to coin what has become my favorite saying over the years:

"Ain't I lucky that my trout can't read the textbook."

As we were arguing, a beautiful blue heron, with a six-to-seven-foot wingspan, settled down on the pond. The fishery expert advised me seriously that we had to trap the heron and move it away; then, tongue in cheek, he advised me that if we weren't going to bother to trap them, we had better shoot them, because a family of blue herons and good trout culture are mutually exclusive.

Next came the forestry man. After walking through the forest with him and receiving valuable guidance, I proudly showed him the beaver dams. His reaction was instantaneous: "Trap them or shoot them. Beavers are the greatest threat to a good-quality forest."

I am happy to say that the herons, the trout, the beavers and the forest are still co-existing, to my joy, and I hope they will do so for generations to come. On reflection, however, I realize that the experts were right. If you want a "perfect forest," beavers are harmful. If you want ponds with the "maximum trout production," blue herons are a destructive force. But my choice was to accept the imperfect beauty of a balanced natural habitat.

For 60 years now, I have seen the world go by, witnessing and living through social ferments where so-called experts had the perfect solution for the pains of an imperfect world. Yes, they all had their radical solutions:

"Trap them or kill them or regiment them."

The experts left behind them a trail of pain and blood and human misery, but they were never "wrong." If you were to ask them, humanity was wrong. We weren't able to live according to their textbooks.

The present attempt to meddle in social sciences is based on experience and observation of humanity in function. Like plants, humanity is imprinted by biological forces, and any attempt to defy them is condemned to fail.

In nature, truth is always simple and must be expressed simply. The truth is that our social system, which I define as entrepreneurial democracy, is:

the most advanced form of civilization in existence;

in tune with the biological needs of man and the technological evolution invented by him.

The choice that man faces is the imperfect world of freedom with all its pains, or the orderly life of the zoo with its soul-destroying cruelty.

The harmony of our social and economic system with the needs of new technology is the greatest hope for the continued existence of man on earth and in our universe.

The evolution of technology imposes an intercourse between all parts of the earth, with all its nations and multiplicity of customs and stages of evolution. This force of unification is irresistible, and can only be achieved peacefully within a decentralized social system —with a division of power and governed by a co-operative spirit, such as those prevailing within the advanced social system of entrepreneurial democracy.

Ultimately, all effort to achieve a unified world under the supreme authority of autocratic centralized power sooner or later will meet with violent resistance equal or superior to the force of coercion imposed. The last 90 years alone bear the scars of many such encounters.

But these coercive and autocratic powers still exist as a constant threat to freedom and, ultimately, to man's very existence.

Introduction

The Manifesto of Entrepreneurial Democracies

The Definition

The entrepreneurial democracy is a political system in which, in addition to the political freedom of parliamentary democracy, there is also an entrepreneurial freedom in business, science and art, wherein the holders of power are constantly challenged by the newly emerging thoughts of entrepreneurial spirits.

We, the citizens of entrepreneurial democracies, proudly proclaim that our political economic system is the most advanced form of civilization ever attained by humanity.

Entrepreneurial democracy is the highest form of political system because it can only come about by the will of the people. It can exist only by consent of its people and can function only through the honesty and virtue of its people.

Because entrepreneurial democracy is an expression of its people, it can be an everlasting system evolving spiritually with the ideas of its people, and economically with the changing technology invented by its people. This capacity to change makes entrepreneurial democracy a peaceful

1

society where the need for violent radical change is eliminated by the opportunity for peaceful evolution.

The Substance

The substance of entrepreneurial democracy is a division of power within the state. Each component of this fragmented power can function with maximum efficiency only to the detriment of the others. Perfection of the whole is achieved by the equilibrium of the division of power. That is why we find in societies governed as entrepreneurial democracies the best administration of justice, the greatest spiritual freedom and the highest standard of living.

The limitation of political power over individual wealth and entrepreneurial activities is essential to the maintenance of individual freedom. Once the state's political power extends over entrepreneurial activities, all hope of spiritual freedom ends. It makes no difference under which flag or ideology the power is exercised: Fascism, Nazism, socialism, Marxism or capitalism.

The blending of economic power with political power of the state will always thrive on corruption and beget incompetence.

When the separation of powers within entrepreneurial society is complete, the democracy will thrive on the morrality of honesty, beget competence and increase man's capacity to create wealth.

Entrepreneurial democracies are fair and compassionate.

Entrepreneurial democracy recognizes the unlimited diversity of man and the importance of this diversity to the harmonious existence of man on earth. It respects the equality of each person regardless of his or her social position, race, education, sex or creed.

Entrepreneurial democracy also respects the spiritual diversity imprinted in man's conscience just as deeply as the pigments of color in our skin. We proclaim proudly the equality of all, their right to participate to the full extent of their ability in the political and economic process of our societies, regardless of their spiritual conscience.

The widest participation in the political process is essential to the maintenance of the division of power. Centuries of history teach us that whenever the division of power is implemented and vigorously respected in a society, it brings about a respect for human life and the expansion of man's potential for compassion. The division of power in every state and in every society brings out the best in man.

Conversely, in societies where the state consolidates all power in its hands, we find a corresponding increase in man's capacity for brutality. Concentration of power under any flag or under any pretext brings out the worst in man.

Entrepreneurial democracies are hopeful societies.

We proclaim our belief in a better future for all people on earth. We believe that our universe has the capacity and the environment necessary for the indefinite sustenance of life. The only commodities in short supply on earth are freedom and knowledge. We reject the prophets of doom who lacking in vision, continually base their estimates on the past knowledge of man, and a belief in the capacity of entrepreneurial people to expand their knowledge as the need arises.

Entrepreneurial democracies have proven their capacity to produce not only sufficient but abundant essentials for the sustenance of man. The greatest threat to the survival and progress of mankind is not our inability to produce all the essentials of survival but rather the forces of dictatorial powers, who are limiting man's freedom to take care of his needs.

Entrepreneurial democracies freely elect their governments.

We, the citizens of entrepreneurial democracies, elect our representatives and appoint them to serve us, but never to rule over us.

We honor them and entrust them with legislative power to protect our freedom from any concentration of power, whatever it may be, religious, political, industrial or hostile states beyond our borders.

We are keenly aware that our legislators in their diversity represent the multitude of interests of our citizens. The conflicting views and interests arising from their diversity must inevitably lead to compromise. The legislators' decisions may not be completely satisfactory to any of us, but are acceptable to most.

The entrepreneurial democracy is an imperfect form of society, nevertheless proving to be more beneficial to its citizens than any of the "perfect" societies experimented with or professed by others.

Entrepreneurial democracies are aware of the dangers inherent in the power vested in the employees of the state, such as the military, administrators and the police. We develop the skill and exercise the vigilance to ensure that they function in service of the people and not as rulers over the people.

It is the fundamental prerequisite of a prosperous and free society to limit the state to the most basic and essential duties which cannot be performed by independent groups of citizens.

Among all possible concentrations of power, an entrenched bureaucracy is the greatest threat to the freedom and prosperity of the entrepreneurial democracy. Employees of the state continuously press for more power, for more secure tenure under the guise of independence from citizens' interest groups; however, whenever they succeed, they become rulers of societies in the name of the supreme interest of the state, and the people become their serfs.

Entrepreneurial societies represent a small yet expanding island of freedom and prosperity in a sea of billions of otherwise deprived humans.

We extend our love and compassion to all these people and invite all the ruling powers to give their people freedom and accept their diversity. If you love your people, it is the only road toward a better future.

Without freedom there is no motivation. Without motivation there is no pursuit of knowledge, and without knowledge man is nothing but a naked ape—and the cruelest ape of all.

The Promise of A Peaceful World

Entrepreneurial democracies have achieved the maturity to reconcile their national interest with a multitude of nations in the promise of a peaceful world.

The prerequisite for a peaceful world is that within its own borders every state respect and accept the multiple diversity of its citizens and freely accommodate their individual interests.

Only nations living by the tenets of this democratic principle are capable of freely negotiating their national interest with other nations for the benefit of mankind.

Entrepreneurial democracies with an absolute internal division of power are the only hope for a peaceful world.

Part 1

The Basics of Entrepreneurial Democracies

Chapter One

Man and Entrepreneurial Democracy

When we look upon our place in the universe, two overwhelming facts command our attention.

First, whatever our philosophical view of the origin of man, religious or evolutionary, man is the most advanced form of creature on earth.

When we consider this fact, the difference between the theory of the creation of man in seven days by God and the theory of man's evolution over billions of years is really only one of semantics.

Undoubtedly, man is the crown of all living creatures on earth, and, as we explore the universe more and more deeply, it becomes evident that until proven otherwise, he is not only unique on earth, but in the solar system as well, and maybe even beyond it. In recent years, it has become evident that man's future existence is not limited to the earth itself, but extends to the whole solar system. Each and every one of us, according to his religious or evolutionary convictions, can come to his own conclusions.

The diversity of man is essential to the harmonious existence of man.

Second, we have to be impressed by the diversity of life on earth and the infinite diversity of man himself.

When we closely examine even the most similar creatures, we find tangible evidence of very subtle differences. The differences in men's spiritual natures are far more significant. Whatever our personal philosophical view of creation, we must accept the fact that the diversity of life, and the diversity of man himself, is essential to his harmonious existence.

It is through this awareness that we recognize the importance and equality of value of every person on earth, regardless of his or her social position, race, education or creed.

Entrepreneurial democracy recognizes the unlimited diversity of man and the unlimited diversified needs for man's happiness. It is the fundamental spirit of entrepreneurial democracy that recognizes the individual's right not only to quality of life but to happiness.

Some of us are compulsive creators and some of us are compulsive loafers.

Some of us, in order to be happy, have to live in an environment that is primitive in nature, or in small isolated communities. Some of us like to live among the crowds in active and bustling cities. Some of us are compulsive creators and workers, and some of us are compulsive loafers.

In entrepreneurial democracies, the diversity of needs for the attainment of happiness is recognized, and people are permitted to live in an environment of their choosing with the opportunity to strive toward their own goals.

The fundamental acceptance of man's equality and the value placed on every single life is the moral foundation on which entrepreneurial democracies are built. The citizens of entrepreneurial democracies, regardless of whether they arrive at this understanding from a religious or an evolutionary conviction, accept the concept of the equality and the importance of each individual human being. These individual rights, enshrined in the laws and the constitutions of the entrepreneurial democracies, are the expression of the spiritual concepts of the great majority of their people.

There is no form of society immune to undesirable diversity.

We must also recognize that man's diversity extends to qualities that we deplore, and for this reason a certain limitation on freedom is expected. For instance, the child molester has an uncontrollable desire which we deplore, and which results in our limiting his freedom. There are also people who infringe upon the freedoms of others through robbing and stealing whenever the opportunity presents itself, without any moral limitation.

It is evident that these unfavorable qualities can be found in all people regardless of nationality, religion, education or social background. There is no form or type of human life that is immune to this undesirable diversity. Naturally, we must accept a limitation on the freedom to express these forms of diversity, and these are the only limits on freedom that are morally justifiable and acceptable in an entrepreneurial democratic society.

Entrepreneurial democracy is the highest form of civilization.

There can be only one valid measure of civilization, and this is the respect by a society for the individual. If we doubt this for one minute, we have but to look upon the events of the last half-century and ask the question: Are certain societies considered civilized, such as those with highly advanced technological knowledge, such as the past national socialism of Germany, with its extermination camps, or the present Marxist regime, whose citizens are deprived of the most elementary prerequisite of civilized existence —the freedom to leave the country at will? No! We must accept that technology by itself does not constitute an advanced civilization.

When we look at the last 5,000 years of the history of man, in spite of all the bright peaks and dark valleys, we must be in awe of our accomplishments. We can think back to just 2,000 years ago, when Roman society featured amphitheaters catering to the public's amusement with the feeding of Christians to lions and gladiator fights. Then we can look upon today's world in which we condemn by law cock fights and debate strenuously the right to life of even the most hardened vicious criminals. We must recognize that entrepreneurial man slowly, and sometimes by tortuous roads, is reaching a higher and higher form of society, which is dominated by compassion and respect for individual life.

Division of power increases man's potential for compassion.

Dictatorial power increases man's capacity for brutality.

The history of this century provides us with a lesson to remember, which is simply that whenever the division of power is implemented and vigorously respected in a nation, the consequence is an increase of individual freedom for all human beings in all their diversity, a rise in respect for human life and the expansion of man's potential for compassion.

Conversely, in nations or societies where the state consolidates all power in its hands, decreasing individual freedoms, we see the increase of man's capacity for brutality and the erosion of his capacity for compassion.

Simply stated, the conclusion is inescapable:

The division of power in each state and each society brings out the best in man.

The concentration of power under any flag, under any pretext brings out the worst in man.

This phenomenon is simple to understand. Dictatorial regimes can exist only through the power of coercion, and coercion creates an insatiable desire for security. In every case, autocratic rulers live in a state of subconscious fear, and fear is brutalizing and dehumanizing to the spirit, thus increasing man's capacity for brutality.

In entrepreneurial society, power is self-liquidating.

In the entrepreneurially free democratic society, every position of power is self-liquidating. Whatever the origin of power, political or industrial, it is temporary in nature and is continually challenged by perpetual change and evolution. Because this is so much a part of the system, it provides a feeling of security which increases man's capacity for generosity and compassion.

For all the diversity of man, we can still discern the existence of two basic characteristics that are found in all races and in all societies, regardless of their level of social structure. It is represented in a gross oversimplification as the nature of active and passive personalities.

The **passive** personality has an overwhelming need for security and a tendency to be extremely conservative, and looks upon evolution with distrust and fear.

Those with **active** personalities need the challenge of change for their happiness. They look upon change with excitement; they are creative and, at worst, can be dominating.

Mankind is continually torn between the forces advocating these choices. In entrepreneurial democracies, these two types of personalities complement each other and find an equilibrium beneficial to everyone.

Since entrepreneurial democracies can function only by the will of their people, conflicting views and interests arising from the diversity of human nature must inevitably be accommodated.

Entrepreneurial democracies are an imperfect form of society, which have nevertheless proven to be more beneficial to mankind than any of the extreme perfections experimented with or professed by others.

The choice of mankind is between the perfect orderly life of the zoos imposed by autocracy or the imperfect freedom of democracy.

Chapter Two

The Substance of Entrepreneurial Democracy

The perfection of entrepreneurial democracy is achieved by the imperfection of its components.

The political system of the parliamentary democracy, with its free entrepreneurial economic system, is the most advanced form ever attained by humanity. All of us who live in these states, without exception, benefit from the highest standard of physical and spiritual freedom ever experienced by man.

> **Entrepreneurial democracy is the highest form of socio-political system because it can only come about by the will of the people. It can exist only by consent, and can function only by the honesty and virtue of its people.**

Because a democracy is an expression of its people, it can be an everlasting system: it is continuously in tune and evolves spiritually with the current thought of its people, and it can evolve economically as changing technology dictates.

The entrepreneurial economic system within a democracy is a progressive and advanced economic form which is in constant evolution, wherein the holders of economic power are constantly challenged by the spirit of newly emerging entrepreneurs.

Entrepreneurial pursuits create wealth, but they also create power. Entrepreneurial democracies recognize that it is essential to limit wealth, particularly the temptation to utilize wealth as power. The substance of entrepreneurial democracy can be expressed and understood as a three-dimensional division of powers within a social system. Each component of this division limits the power of the other. The division may be expressed as:

> **the limitation of political power over the judiciary;**
>
> **the limitation of political power over economic wealth;**
>
> **and the limitation of wealth over the political powers.**

The progress and survival of democracy depend on the continual fine tuning, through legislative action, of the equilibrium of these multi-directional forces.

Because our democracies have successfully survived over two centuries, we consider them to be the natural state of existence, and we tend to overlook the importance of each of these three-dimensional forces. The division of political power and the limits it imposes on our individual wealth is undergoing serious erosion, because the clarity of our judgment has been clouded by the pervasive socialist Marxist influence in the last half-century.

We see, day after day, devoted supporters of democracy willing to fight any encroachment of political power on the judiciary, look with complete indifference at the spectacle of political power encroaching upon individual wealth and state control over entrepreneurial freedom.

These people fail to realize that once a state's political power controls entrepreneurial economic activities, all hope of spiritual freedom simultaneously vanishes. It makes no difference under which flag or ideological pretense the power of domination is exercised —Fascism, Nazism or Marxism —once control and direction of entrepreneurial activities are vested in political power. These political powers are so dominant over the daily activities of men that all spiritual freedom ceases to exist, and separation of the judiciary from the state is nothing but a dead letter of the constitution.

Conversely, the substance and progress of democracy are also jeopardized by the blind force of entrepreneurial wealth. In the name of efficiency, these entrepreneurial powers continually gravitate toward the creation of powerful trusts in order to completely dominate their particular segments of the market. They fail to recognize that today's absolute efficiency is the road to tomorrow's inefficiency. The concept that total efficiency is achieved by total control of the market is a mirage, and pursuing it is destructive. The ideology of the organization —entrepreneurial or state-controlled—is unimportant once total control is achieved. It becomes political, in direct conflict with the entrepreneurial needs of democracy, and becomes a destructive force in that democracy.

The life of wealth created by the entrepreneurial spirit goes through formative, adult and old-age periods no different from human beings. In its youth, it is adventurous, inventive and challenging. We can call this period the formative years. Adulthood is the most productive period, producing wealth in a continuous process. With the aging process, the entrepreneurial spirit loses its inventiveness and looks to convert its wealth to power, in order to protect itself from the challenge of emerging new wealth.

In most cases, by the old-age phase, the direction and control of the wealth have been transferred from its creators to the hands of administrative and bureaucratic-oriented management. In this stage, it starts to closely resemble state-run socialist enterprises. This new generation, born in the comfort and security of wealth, often lacks the feeling of security and strength of its predecessors and tries to preserve its position not by the vigor of its creativeness, but by converting wealth into political power.

Entrepreneurial democracies can survive only by maintaining conditions that limit the political power of wealth and make it vulnerable to emerging new entrepreneurs.

Entrepreneurial democracies are the highest form of socio-political system because they can control and maintain not only a division of political power, but also a division of wealth and economic power. The capacity of our society to maintain this division is illustrated eloquently in the history of the automotive industry in the United States. For a number of years, the development of advanced technology and production methods represented by this industry offered its workers the highest standard of living ever experienced by a labor force. During its years of adulthood, from the 1940s to the early 1960s, it was the greatest creator of wealth not only for its owners but for the community in which it functioned. In the 1970s, the symptoms of old age manifested themselves—the loss of inventiveness, the incapacity to change and the increased attempts to function by throwing around wealth as political power.

For a few years, the automotive industry, and the steel industry, which was closely connected with it, functioned under the principle of "the captive market," and not of competitive strength. It was a cozy arrangement, benefitting first the bureaucratic administration, and next the unions, but it was of dubious benefit to the shareholders as owners, and it was detrimental to the general public and ultimately the industry itself.

In spite of the immense economic power that the automotive industry represented, the political forces of the state were strong enough to allow the inflow of automobiles from other countries, mainly Germany and Japan, which had a more vigorous entrepreneurial spirit.

Another meaningful challenge to the industrial power base was the environmental-control legislation. When it became evident that the old design of automobiles represented a public danger because it polluted the atmosphere, concern for this problem was disseminated and constantly maintained in the public consciousness by the media.

The immense power of the automotive industry and the revenue which it represented to the media through the advertising industry could not silence the concerns expressed by citizens, who, through political pressure, brought about legislated mandatory changes in the design of the automobile, such as the pollution-control catalytic converter. This is a most gratifying example of the division of power that is essential to the progress and survival of entrepreneurial democracy.

It is a great credit to the parliamentarians and the statesmen of those democracies, including Japan's, that they moderated the challenge to the automotive industry by legislation strong enough to induce it to look for improved productivity and technical know-how, but not so strong that the industry was destroyed, with all the consequential human suffering that such an event would inevitably have caused.

The third dimension of entrepreneurial democracy, the power of the judiciary, also has its destructive elements. There are those who constantly press for increased judiciary power, in the name of efficiency, in their fight against criminal elements in our society. These people fail to recognize that historically, whenever the state has accorded excess power to the judiciary, the latter has become more oppressive and arbitrary than the criminal element from which it was supposed to protect us.

The perfection of entrepreneurial democracy is found, paradoxically, in the imperfection of its components.

Each component can achieve maximum efficiency only to the detriment of the others.

Perfection is achieved by the equilibrium of the division of power.

Hence, we find in a society governed by entrepreneurial democracy the best administration of justice, the greatest spiritual freedom and the highest standard of living.

Chapter Three

The Morality of Entrepreneurial Democracy

The essential criterion for success in an entrepreneurial society is respect for honesty and truth.

It is a pervasive thought in our society that entrepreneurial activities are directed by dishonesty and greed. The socialist ideologists have been partially responsible for this defamation, and, as with all lies, if it is repeated often enough it becomes accepted as truth.

The source of this falsehood is, however, more deep-seated. It can be explained by a fundamental split in human nature, specifically, the active and the passive natures of man (see Chapter One).

After the formative years, when every individual has to choose a career, each and every one of us naturally tries to find a vocation and environment fitting our personality—where happiness may best be achieved. Those with an active nature usually find entrepreneurial and challenging endeavors in the fields of science, art or business. Those of a more passive nature look for security and gravitate toward secure administrative pursuits in state-controlled activities.

The choice is the security of servitude or the uncertainty of freedom.

Because our desire for freedom is an overpowering force, some people rationalize their self-denial of freedom by saying, "I do not have a tough enough skin or morality to join the rat race." In reality, what they most often do not have is the courage or self-assurance to face the uncertainty, or simply the desire to face challenges.

Those with passive personalities most often have an unjustified inferior self-image. This misplaced self-image is rationalized by a paranoid view of the entrepreneurial world.

The reality is just the opposite. To succeed in any entrepreneurial endeavour, either science, art or business, whether individually or as part of an organization, **the most essential criterion for success is a very basic respect for honesty and truth.**

In entrepreneurial societies, the interest in survival imposes the morality of honesty.

In state-controlled societies, the interest of survival imposes corruption.

In the entrepreneurial environment, falsehoods are destructive. The reasons for this may seem obscure, but they are easy to understand.

- Entrepreneurial business activities can survive only when they generate profit and additional wealth. Consequently, all entrepreneurial activity is directed toward the most cost-efficient form.
- Every dishonest action or possible action imposes additional imposition of controls, with their non-productive cost.
- In every entrepreneurial activity, the non-productive costs are administrative controls.

The forces of self-preservation and self-interest, similar to the irresistible force of gravity, move relations between entrepreneurial entities toward honesty, both in relation to each other and within themselves.

Consequently, entrepreneurial entities can function efficiently only in an environment of mutual trust, truth and honesty. This is true for their relations within the organization, in relation to each other and with their customers.

In an entrepreneurial democracy, the entrepreneur has only one power—to sell his product or services. He counts on the will and desire of his customers to use his product. He has no power to impose on them. He can use the power of advertising, but advertising is powerful and beneficial only when it is honest and not misleading. Nobody has ever created meaningful wealth by selling a product or service which did not stand up to the scrutiny of its market.

Honesty in the entrepreneurial environment is as powerful as gravity, but just as we can escape gravity by the powerful thrust of rockets, so can the attraction of honesty be annulled and compensated for by other forces.

One example is when man's entrepreneurial activities escape the laws of competition and the need for honesty by the creation of captive markets.

Another example is catering to powerful customers, such as the state or other institutions, who defy the laws of competition because the performance of those in power is not evaluated by well-defined criteria and can therefore escape the consequences of mismanagement.

In a competitive environment, the interest in survival imposes on an entrepreneurial society the morality of honesty.

In a state-controlled society, the interest in survival breeds corruption. This is true regardless of the political nature of the state, whether it is an absolute monarchy or a Marxist state.

It has long been observed that power corrupts. Once again, the reasons are obscure but can be easily understood. In the social and economic environment, where the state has overwhelming power, the state can exercise its power only by controls.

- Controls are exercised by administrative functions.
- Administrative control is a bureaucratic function, and not a wealth-producing creative function.
- In this environment, the power shifts from the wealth-producing leadership to the bureaucratic leadership.
- The power of honesty is nullified. As the power base is shifted to controls, self-motivating forces push for the growth and expansion of controls.
- Bureaucratic power increases with the assumed need of its functions.
- When political and economic power is vested in the state, the political consideration is always the strongest. Thus, the power of control is given to those who will reliably serve political interests, and not to the most competent.

Competence can be measured by performance. Political reliability can be judged only by intimate knowledge of a person. Political reliability is an undefined value judgment giving unlimited power to the decision maker. It is beneficial only to those holding power and to those who are close to the holders of power.

The blending of economic power with political power of the state always thrives on corruption and begets incompetence.

An example of this occurred when the spiritual and political powers of the churches were extended over entrepreneurial activity. To bring back the Christian morality of the church, it was essential to deprive it of the power of wealth. Conversely, for wealth to function in honesty, it has to be freed from the power of the state or the church.

When separation of powers within an entrepreneurial democracy is complete; the democracy will thrive in the morality of honesty, and will beget competence and increase its capacity to create wealth.

The division of economic and political powers in a state will increase its wealth-creating potential and will enhance the individual spiritual freedom and the physical well-being of man.

We can learn how creative vigor can be drained from a society from the history of England. With the aging of the wealthy enterprises created after the industrial revolution, the leadership of those enterprises shifted from the most competent to the most reliable (or those perceived as reliable) under the class system.

This system permeated advancement in industry, politics and the army. Those who were perceived as trustful were raised to power not by virtue of their competence, but based on their class.

The consequences of this are evident. We have observed the erosion of the wealth-creating power of England, which caused it to rapidly sink to one of the lowest standards of living in Western Europe, where before it had provided one of the highest standards of living.

In conjunction with the development of the class system created by the power of wealth, the labor force evolved toward radicalization. The evolution of the English labor movement is a classic example of how the behavior of the labor force and unions is nothing more than a mirror image of the behavior of management.

When management operates in the spirit of entrepreneurial competence and honesty, the labor force always reacts favorably in a spirit of cooperation. Competent leadership creates trust and motivates the rank and file, like an army under competent and committed leadership, which often acts heroically and beyond the call of duty.

Conversely, as incompetent generals will dispirit the strongest army, so incompetent management creates mistrust and hostility among those in the labor force, who see the hope of upward mobility for their children only in the destruction of the system. This creates a relationship of hostility in lieu of cooperation.

Positive examples of entrepreneurial democracies are seen in the evolution of West Germany and Japan. Their success can be attributed to many factors, but in both cases the influence of two factors is inescapable:

- The existing class system was destroyed through military defeat.
- The bureaucratic infrastructure, with its power to obstruct and limit entrepreneurial activities, was also destroyed.

From the ruins emerged a new society where those who were the most competent and creative were able to direct, without bureaucratic controls, the wealth and prosperity of their nation. They have provided an example of a miracle of the creative potential of a free society. In both nations we have also seen the cooperative relationship between management and the rank-and-file labor force, who perceive management as competent and committed to success for the benefit of all.

Certainly, we all know, or should know, that the limit of man's potential for creativity is difficult to fathom. Unquestionably, the ravages of war, which we hope will never be experienced by today's generation, released creative forces which could only have flourished in the total freedom of the resulting political vacuum.

It is certain that Germany's and Japan's challenge to the rest of the industrial world will diminish in direct proportion to the increase in bureaucratic forces of these states and to the success of the new wealth in limiting the challenge of the up-and-coming entrepreneurial spirit.

Following the military defeat of Nazi Germany and imperial Japan, the people of these nations inflicted an even greater and more significant defeat on their autocratic rulers. To justify the brutal oppression of all of those opposed to their power, these self-appointed saviors predicted the enslavement of their nation as a consequence of military defeat.

The example of the Japanese and the German people has proven that what people need is not generals and dictators, but freedom. Once freedom is attained and the entrepreneurial and creative forces are given free rein, every nation shall find its rightful place in association with all other democratic nations.

Part 2

Issues of Entrepreneurial Democracies

Chapter Four

The Anatomy of Profit

Profit is the instrument by which entrepreneurial democracies measure the continuous creation of wealth for the benefit of society.

In the conventional thought of our society, "profit" has the connotation of evil. According to the tenets of socialism, profit has about the same connotation as the evil spirit or devil had for the Christians during the Dark Ages. It is condemned with the same hatred and prejudice. This socialist religion has attributed to profit all the hardships, suffering and shortcomings of our society.

The high priests of this socialist religion are determined to purify our society from the wicked profit-motivated entrepreneur with a zeal reminiscent of the witch-burning inquisitors. Their actions are similiarly devoid of all scientific foundation. They are no different from other religious zealots, except that their action is based solely on dogmas of Marxist theology.

Mankind arrived at his present understanding of the world and the universe by trying to identify their components and define their functions. We should proceed in the same manner with regard to the notion of profit in our society. The judgment on its value to our society should be rendered only after we have identified and defined its function.

What is "profit"?

Profit is the sum of wealth created over and above the sum expended on its creation.

The simplest way to understand this is to go back to the earliest stages of human development.

Once upon a time, when man was still in the hunting/picking stages and sustained himself by gathering enough food to nourish himself, the first entrepreneur was born. This person was not satisfied to simply gather enough grain and berries for his sustenance needs, but collected more and more!

We can safely presume that collecting more made it possible for him to seed the first plot of land. What motivated his action we do not know. Was it that he was restless and continued picking while the rest of the band were sleeping on their full bellies? Or that he ate less, preserving day after day part of his grains and berries? Or was he an extremely strong member of the band who cruelly robbed the weaker? Or was he a noble soul who saw the increasing size of the band and, with enterprising spirit, collected more grain than he needed to meet his immediate needs, so that he was able to sow the first plot of land?

We do not know if this primitive band cultivated and harvested its plot collectively or individually, but it is certain that they created individual or collective profit, in the form of collecting more grain than they consumed in the sustenance of their work to take care of the increasing size of the band to feed. This additional wealth of grain took care of the increasing size of the band by producing additional yields, thereby creating additional wealth.

> **Every step in the improvement of man's ability to sustain himself and improve his lot has been achieved by generating additional wealth over and above the needs of his sustenance.**

We can move rapidly by travelling thousands of years to when the first man with an entrepreneurial spirit designed a plow. There were members of the band who had very special skills in working with wood and, later, in working with metal, and we can be certain that those who made use of these craftsmen's skills paid for them with grain and other essential goods.

The master craftsman's profit for his labor was the additional goods received over and above his needs, which allowed him to trade for animals, wool and perhaps wood to build his first dwelling.

The primitive farmer who traded part of his grain for a plow also hoped to make a profit by being able to increase his grain production, reduce the cost of his labor and produce more with the help of the new tool that he had paid for in grain.

From the earliest primitive time to our present complicated structure of society, generation of profit is nothing more than the creation of wealth. As mankind grows in numbers, the desire to improve our lot and daily lives can only be accomplished by the growth and preservation of wealth. As our society evolved from the primitive barter system, profit became abstract and more difficult to comprehend, **but profit is and will always be an essential component of the betterment of life on earth**.

Along with "profit," "capital" is probably the most despised word in the hate literature of the socialist dogma. To understand the function of capital is easy. Obviously, it is nothing more than the preservation of wealth created by profit.

When we think about capital, we think of dollar signs and money in general, but capital is not money. Money by itself has no value. It is a promissory note developed by our civilization as a means by which wealth and services can be traded, bought and sold. The need to create capital in any society becomes obvious as soon as we understand this.

We are aware that nothing is permanent in our universe — not even the strongest marble or concrete palaces, steel and plastic. Everything is subjected to a process of continuous deterioration by oxidation. Thus, even a society that does not want to increase its standard of living is forced, just to preserve it, to generate profit and accumulate wealth (capital) to replace its crumbling and ever-decreasing wealth.

The issue facing us today is not whether our society can exist without profit and increasing capital (without it man would regress to the berry-picking stage). The issue is, can we, or should we, generate profit in a society based on the desires and decisions of its individual members, or should we do so under a socialist system, which imposes its collective values on its own members?

During the course of our long history, unfortunately, profit generated by the inventiveness and creativeness of man has been expropriated for the benefit of monarchs, Caesars, lords and religious leaders serving gods or imperial states under a wide variety of names.

In substance they were all the same, appropriating and confiscating all profit wealth created by their subjects for their own personal benefit or for the benefit of the empire as they perceived it. In every instance, their subjects were left with only the bare essentials. Since they were completely destitute, they were deprived of all capacity to influence the use of the wealth generated by their creativeness. History tells us about enlightened monarchs in many parts of the world who used their power of confiscation with discretion, realizing that **man's capacity to invent or create increases in direct proportion to the benefits retained from toil and individual decision-making freedom in the use of those benefits.**

Individual, spiritual freedom and the right to ownership of tangible goods have always proceeded hand in hand throughout our long history.

Throughout the evolution of technology, man's ability to create and invent became more and more essential to the enrichment of the state and society as a whole. Consequently, his freedom became more essential. This brought about a steady growth in the number of people who had the right to own wealth.

> **With the right to ownership of material wealth, we observe a corresponding increase in the dignity of man and of his physical and spiritual freedom.**

During the time of the industrial revolution, there were still masses living in total destitution, who were also deprived of their most essential spiritual freedoms. Their suffering and inferior status formed the spring which influenced the development of the ideology usually referred to as Marxism or socialism. They erroneously came to the conclusion that most of the population had been deprived of the benefits of their labor because of the individual ownership of wealth. They advocated ownership of all wealth by the state, without realizing that this is not an evolutionary advance. It is in fact the turning back of the clock by simply replacing the power of the monarch who said "I am the state" with the power of individuals saying "We are the people."

Fortunately, there were others who realized and believed that the **solution to man's inhumanity to man is not found in the concentration of power but in the division of power.** This was the quintessence of the philosophy that gave birth to British parliamentary monarchy and the French and American revolutions and that guided the evolution of Western European absolute monarchies toward constitutional or parliamentary monarchies.

History, ancient and recent, proves through empirical experience that there is a symbiotic relationship between the right to ownership of tangible wealth and man's individual dignity and spiritual freedom.

The limitation of the power of the state to confiscate wealth has a chain-reaction effect just as powerful as nuclear energy.

The right to ownership raises man's dignity.

Dignity increases the desire for the pursuit of knowledge; knowledge creates invention and improves technology, which creates increased wealth, and so on.

Democracy and entrepreneurial freedom create the potential and the will to elevate man from a beast to a compassionate and caring human being. As wealth spreads to more individuals, and the very basic needs of education, shelter and care of the aged are secured, and as man's right and capacity to participate in the political process increases, man feels more secure; fear, the most destructive force and the origin of inhumanity, is reduced, if not completely eliminated.

On the other hand, socialist Marxist economic systems have the potential to impoverish man physically and, inevitably, spiritually. This process of impoverishment of society as a whole is only temporarily overshadowed by the assistance provided to society's most destitute.

Today, the failure of the socialist systems is forestalled by the constant inflow into those states of the benefits and creativeness from the entrepreneurial democracies. This inflow is manifested not only in the billions and billions of dollars in loans and assistance provided by these nations to the socialist states, but also by the inflow of technological advances that are made possible by the ever-expanding body of scientific knowledge produced by a free society. Without their support, and even in spite of their support, socialist Marxist states are slowly but inevitably sinking toward the level of the undeveloped nations. History provides us with numerous examples of the destructive effect of confiscation of wealth on the strengths and potentials of a nation.

Nothing is more instructive than the history of the Spanish empire. In the late 1400s, Spain was a respected state by all accounts; its knowledge of science and the freedom of its citizens, equalled those of any nation, including France and England. The use of the power of the inquisition as a means to confiscate the wealth of its citizens of Jewish and Muslim origin went hand in hand with restrictions on the freedom of thought of all its citizens. The confiscation proceeded under the guise of Christianity, but the fact that it extended to all converts, and beyond them to the group of Marranos who had converted from Judaism generations earlier, clearly indicates that religion was only a pretext. In reality, the motivation was to confiscate wealth.

In the same period, England, Holland and Germany accorded to an increasing number of their citizens the right to ownership and individual wealth. Legislators enshrined these rights in their laws. The exploding creative capacity of these nations resulted in a continuous rise in the standard of living, an expansion in creativity, knowledge and science, resulting in technological advances and the emergence of those nations as the most powerful states in the world. At the same time, slowly but inevitably, Spain and the other nations where the inquisition retained its power were sinking into the dark ages of obscurity.

The accelerated speed with which science evolves in our time makes this process visible within a few decades instead of centuries. Only the continuous inflow of wealth and knowledge generated by the entrepreneurial democracies moderates the speed of decline of Marxist socialist nations.

Chapter Five

Technology and Freedom

For the peaceful coexistence of society, it is essential that the political system be in tune with the state of its technology.

State-controlled societies governed by socialist doctrines are in direct conflict with the division of power imposed by the miniaturization of technology.

The Effect of Miniaturization

The most important dominating force in the evolution of our present technology is its miniaturization. State-controlled societies directed by socialist doctrines are in direct conflict with the division of power and the instant decision-making capacity imposed by miniaturization. As such, they are condemned by the evolutionary forces; they are a reactionary and conservative system, and they are the greatest source of potential friction to the peaceful coexistence of man.

Marxist theologians predicted the inevitability of the evolution of mankind toward the socialist system, in which all means of production would be owned by the state. They believed that the evolution of technology would impose larger and larger production units, because the larger the unit the more efficient its production. The free and entrepreneurial society was supposed to be left with only two choices:

- to evolve toward the larger production unit, which would result in a dominant position of the owners over the individuals in society, provoking revolution and state ownership of the means of production; or

- to preserve a multitude of inefficient production units, which would bring about an inferior living standard compared to Marxist societies, again provoking revolution fueled by the desire for a better standard of living.

This philosophical and quasi-religious conviction was the motivating force behind Marxist states' commitment to create giant industrial complexes and agricultural combines.

The miniaturization of technology by entrepreneurial society is the tangible evidence that Marxist theory is nothing but a reactionary dogma developed on the evidence of 19th-century theology by men unable to understand the forces of changing technology created by entrepreneurial democracy.

One of the best examples of the effect of miniaturization is found in the history of the bread-baking industry.

At the time of the birth of industrial society, the production of bread was one of the most difficult and time-consuming physical labors. The industrial revolution brought about bread factories. For only two or three decades, giant bread factories represented an advanced means of production in comparison to neighborhood bakeries. However, they had their shortcomings. To justify the cost of the machinery, they became efficient only with very high production. The large production unit demanded distribution over a large district far from the point of production, with an inevitable increase in complexity of logistics, and with increasing amounts of spoilage.

As the distance increased between the production point and consumption point, production became less sensitive to the needs of consumers. England was one of the first states to engineer and implement bread factories. France and, to a lesser degree, Germany, where the quality of the bread and the relationship between the family bakery and the public was more important than its cost efficiency, advanced to a lesser degree. For a few decades, the means of bread production in England was more advanced and less costly than that in France or Germany. The miniaturization of technology in the baking industry, however, made the large bread factories obsolete and inefficient. In the last few decades, we have seen the individual neighborhood bakery acquire a means of production which, to a large degree, has eliminated the hard physical work. We have seen labor-saving equipment installed even in the smallest privately owned bakeries.

Today, these miniaturized industrial bakeries represent the most efficient means of bread production. The individual neighborhood bakery now has no need for packaging, no need for enormous investment or for energy use in the logistics of distribution. The owner has an intimate knowledge of the needs of his customers which enables him to minimize spoilage.

> **Because of his small size and his ability to make instant decisions without any bureaucratic hindrance, he is able to implement all the improvements in production methods offered by the constant evolution of new technology.**

Today, the small neighborhood bakery of the entrepreneurial society not only represents a more advanced and efficient system in comparison with socialized or privately owned bread factories, but also offers more satisfying working conditions to the labor force. Working on the automated production lines of the bread factory represented an improvement over the hard toil of manual bread making. However, when compared to the neighborhood bakery working conditions, which offer the participant the satisfaction of decision making and the joy of creative participation in the quality of the end product, bread-factory working conditions may be regarded as dehumanizing and barbaric.

Baking is only one of the many industries where the miniaturization of technology resulted in an advanced and more efficient form of production. Agriculture is another industry where miniaturization has achieved great advances. The harvester combine is no more than the miniaturization of the harvester, the binder and the threshing machine. The corn harvester, the roto-tiller and the auto-feed auger for beef and chicken farms are examples of highly efficient miniaturization of tools with which entrepreneurial society created the miracle of abundance. This miniaturization of equipment made it possible for thousands of small farm units to efficiently specialize in one segment of the chain of food production.

The transport truck, with its removable container, is another example of miniaturization, as it has taken over a large segment of the transportation of goods from the railroad industry. The calculator, the computer and communication equipment are all the harbingers of the coming age of miniaturization. The greatest impact will come within the next 20 to 30 years, when technology will achieve the miniaturization of the power plant—when every household, every farm and every industrial plant will control its own source of energy. The giant power plants will be nothing more than relics of the past.

Miniaturization will render obsolete today's education centers. Miniaturization of communication equipment will bring about an explosion of education, providing knowledge in delight and diversity beyond our imaginations. Decentralized power, decentralized decision making, and a decentralized education system will result in an inevitable change toward a decentralized political system.

The dogmatic, socialistic economic and political systems are built on centralized power, which is in direct conflict with evolution, and as such are reactionary systems condemned by historical forces.

Whenever a political social system is in direct conflict with the needs of advanced technology, it is condemned to oblivion. The inferior capacity of this society to produce goods and wealth renders it a weaker member of the world community. Sooner or later it will be dominated by the more advanced and stronger states where the political systems are in tune with the needs of advanced technology.

The reactionary forces of socialist dogma can temporarily impose their will on society; they can retard and postpone the advance of mankind, but they cannot stop it.

> **Reactionary forces can never permanently alter the history of mankind, they can only increase the amount of blood and tears spilled on the road to progress.**

New Electronic Information

When historians of future generations review the 20th century, it will clearly emerge as a crucial period in society's progress, entailing gigantic struggles between the forces of enlightened truth and freedom and the oppressive dogmatic forces —Nazism, Fascism and Marxism. It is hoped that the 20th century will be also remembered as the century of victory by man's rational enlightenment and cooperative forces. Otherwise there will be no more history.

> **The evolution of technology has made the victory of enlightened cooperation irresistible.**

Next to miniaturization, society's new electronic information capacity is the strongest technological force for the destruction of centralized power systems of dictatorial regimes.

The dogma of Marxism can be compared to the 17th century science of alchemy. For centuries, man tried unsuccessfully to penetrate the secret of the chemistry of the universe. During those centuries, alchemists theorized and produced libraries of literature, without resolving the mystery of matter and without achieving any of their objectives, among them the transmutation of base metals into gold and a universal remedy for all maladies.

Man's inventiveness created the microscope, and with it unveiled the secret of fungi and bacteria. Microscopes helped in the advancement of the science of chemistry by unveiling the secret of molecules, and made alchemy obsolete.

The alchemists tried to understand the chemical make-up of our world, and we can only admire their persistence and inquisitiveness, and say with admiration how much they learned with so little means at their disposal. Similarly, we can only have admiration for the early Marxist theorists, who were undoubtedly motivated by the finest humanitarian intentions, which found their roots in our Judeo-Christian heritage of compassion for man's hardships and suffering. Although we can respect their intention, we can deplore the dogmatism of their proposed remedies.

The computer has the effect the microscope had on alchemy. In the late 19th century and early 20th century, Marxists found it easy to state that depriving the rich of their wealth would alleviate all human misery. Today, this type of rationale cannot work. Through the use of the computers we can rapidly see how much wealth exists and can prove mathematically that its distribution to the poorer masses would be just a drop in the bucket.

When we talk about the inadequacy of the taxation system, we are able to calculate instantly the number of households and their earnings. We can determine with exactitude the possible increase in the standard of living for the average family upon confiscation of this wealth, and can calculate the resultant decline in productivity arising from this action.

When we submit the inequities existing in our world to the examination of this new "microscope," the computer, the inequities between rich and poor nations or the inequities among the people of a nation, the evidence clearly emerges that **no redistribution of existing wealth can raise the living standard of the poor; only the creation of new wealth can do so.**

When we submit the wealth-creating capacity of entrepreneurial democracies to the inspection of this new instrument of technology and compare it to a similar inspection of state-controlled societies, we clearly see that the wealth-creating capacity of entrepreneurial democracy and its capability to distribute the essential needs of people are far superior to those in any Marxist state, be it moderate socialist or extreme Marxist. There is no need to compare

Japan, Taiwan and Hong Kong, or even the Philippines, to Communist China. The comparison of East Germany, Poland, Czechoslovakia and Romania to West Germany, Belgium and Holland speaks for itself.

In addition to the computer, we also have electronic communication, which imposes on nations a discipline that cannot be obscured by dogmatic propaganda. Today, we have the capacity to calculate the productivity of every nation and its balance-of-trade deficits or gains. In spite of all the work of dogmatic propaganda, the reality imposes rational solutions and discipline on every nation. Those who ignore it face the peril of bankruptcy and destitution.

State-controlled societies make a supreme effort to hide the reality from their people. Because the truth is unacceptable, they have to maintain a strict limitation on the flow of information, which is in direct conflict with the information needs of our new technological society.

The strict censorship of all thoughts opposing or disagreeing with their dogmatic view of the world, the limits imposed on the freedom of their citizens to travel and see the world and to reflect on evidence beyond that preached by party headquarters, will force them into more and more accelerated isolation or desperate adventurism to destroy and challenge truth.

Ultimately, the focus of technology always wins. The new technology requires diversification of information, which is in direct conflict with the needs of the dictatorial state for central control of information.

Chapter Six

The Virtue of Multinationals

The multinational organization acts as a catalyst for and conciliator of the conflicting national interests of nations.

No other institution of entrepreneurial democracies is hated more by the apostles of socialism than the multinational institution. When we listen to the invective thrown at them even by more moderate socialist or liberal thinkers, it is evident that they have become the favorite whipping boys of our society.

In their home countries, they are cursed because they export capital and work-creating enterprises. In the countries where the enterprises are set up, they are cursed because they retain the power of management of the same enterprises. In reality, what makes them so hateful is that they are the precursor and avant garde of a world to come, and, like all other innovative and evolutionary institutions, they are the product of entrepreneurial democracies.

**The salient characteristic of multinationals
is not the power or wealth but "know-how."
Whatever we perceive as power is, in fact,
the strength of their special knowledge.**

Knowledge is a strength which cannot be coerced by political forces. One can expropriate tools and factories, but not knowledge.

This capacity of resistance to political coercion makes multinationals so hateful to political forces. Because knowledge cannot be coerced, the political powers of states are forced to compromise and moderate their strength in exercising their power.

The Soviet Union does not invite Fiat or Pepsi to organize car factories or soft-drink bottling plants because of their riches, but because of their unique know-how. China invites the multinational oil companies to explore the China Sea not because of their power of wealth, but because of their know-how.

A multinational enterprise is simply an organization of people devoted, with expertise and creative energy, to producing profit and wealth through a specific product needed by mankind. Because they operate in many countries, their leaders are drawn from many nationalities and develop a solidarity beyond their national and genetic origin, and often escape the restrictive forces of old national political power. As the rapidly expanding systems of communication and travel shrink the world and make national borders obsolete, the multinationals should be regarded as the beacon of hope for a better and more peaceful world to come on earth.

Man working for multinational organizations can retain his love and attachment for his people as an individual. However, as his activities inside the organization are concerned with marketing and production, they are not subjected to the narrow interest of his particular national group but are directed toward the interest of the organization as a whole.

The interests and objectives of a multinational organization are no different in substance from those of any other productive enterprise: first, to produce a particular product in the best possible form and quality to meet its customers' needs, and second, to produce it by the most efficient production method. These two objectives are the driving force of every entrepreneurial enterprise, national or multinational, but they are functional only in a free-market environment where they are continuously challenged in the power base by existing or emerging similar enterprises.

We have seen the working of these forces in the emergence of the Japanese- and German-based enterprises challenging the well-established multinationals. Once again, as many times in the past, we see that the entrepreneurial activity, even when it is directed by self-interest and egotistical consideration of one's own group, brings about effects which are totally altruistic and in the interests of all men.

Multinationals have been accused of wielding too much political power. However, it has been proven over and over again that the political power of multinational corporations is a myth. We see small states with no other status but their political power expropriating physical assets of multinationals. Arab sheikdoms have proven to be powerful enough to dictate to and impose their will on the largest multinationals. This can happen simply because they are "multinationals" and no one nation has an absolute vested interest in protecting them. By virtue of their multinational nature, they have a pacifying effect on the conflicting, narrow interests of national states.

Another aspect which makes multinationals so hateful to Marxist and moderate socialists is that their existence and activity are tangible proof of the absurdity of social political theories. Just as entrepreneurial democracies have spread their knowledge and wealth, which has made possible all the social benefits of old-age pensions, unemployment insurance and union-protected labor laws, they have not succumbed to the power of self-interest, as Marxist theory predicted. Similarly, multinationals are breaking out of the self-centered **egotistical will and power of national states to the benefit and welfare of the poor nations.** Once again they are proving that the drive toward the most efficient form and lowest cost of production can be a positive force. After benefitting the individual national state, they now spread their benefit to the whole world.

> **Multinational companies are ahead of their time, and are in direct conflict with the parochial interests of the national politicians.**

All humans and all activities of humans can be misdirected and used in a destructive manner (see Chapter Two). Multi national companies are no exceptions. They can painfully succumb to temptation. Whenever this happens, it is due to the dishonesty of individuals and is in direct conflict with the long-term interests of the enterprise itself.

The basic nature and self-interest of a multinational organization coincides with the interest in material prosperity and spiritual liberty of any nation in which it operates.

Chapter Seven

The Stress of Change

The stress of change is the inevitable price of freedom.

How our institutions or we, as individuals, respond to the stress determines the evolution of society. When exposed to the pain of stress, we look for stability and are willing to sacrifice our freedom, but the price we pay for the so-called stability always proves to be painful to the extreme.

All forms of civilization are exposed to the stresses of evolutionary changes. Entrepreneurial democracies are continuously subjected to stresses created by changing technology. Today, they manifest themselves in two important sectors of our social fabric:

the institution of our education system;

the institution of the family.

The Education System

Stress on our education system manifests itself in chronic unemployment of youth between the ages of 16 and 22.

The symptom is chronic in every advanced free society. It is the consequence of stress between the dynamics of technological changes produced by entrepreneurial activities and the institutionalized education system, which is dominated by the interests of fossilized bureaucratic structures slow to adapt to the present needs of our society.

To understand this, we have to review the history of compulsory education. At first, compulsory education extended only to the fourth grade and varied depending on the degree of technological advancement of each nation.

Just 100 years ago, it was normal for boys and girls to enter the labor force by the age of 10. This acceptable age was gradually increased to 12 or 13, and is now 16. The increase in the acceptable age to enter the labor force evolved in proportion to the increased need for education demanded by new technology, and was made possible only by the increased productivity of that same technology, which created new wealth to pay for the increased cost of education supported by our societies.

To acquire knowledge and understanding of our world and beyond it, the education period should be extended to at least grade 16 or 17 to meet the needs of our future society. Within the next decade or two, to enter the labor force before the age of 18 or 20 will be looked upon as inappropriate.

Up until the early 20th century, education was primarily for the sake of obtaining knowledge. Students learned to read and studied languages to increase their potential and absorb additional knowledge. This relentless pursuit of knowledge made possible the advancement of technology and the miracles of the 19th and 20th centuries.

In the early 20th century, more education was directed toward very specific professions, and it was expected that through this specific education each student would be assured employment in his profession. This job-oriented education has progressed to the preposterous degree of teaching carpentry, welding and auto-body repair in high schools. The new advances in science and technology have made this system obsolete.

> **The new technology does not demand the knowledge of how to do it, but of "why we do it."**

The difference is substantial. The knowledge of "how to do it" will become obsolete with the rapidly changing technology. The knowledge of "why we do it" equips students with the understanding of the consequences of their actions and increases their capacity to adapt to the inevitable changes.

Canada is a good example of our inability to adapt to the needs created by the new technology. Canada's unemployment system permits a young person to leave school at the age of 16, enter the work force for 14 to 20 weeks, depending on the region of Canada, and then be entitled to unemployment benefits for a period of approximately 40 weeks at 60 percent of his weekly earnings. For example, if a person earns $5.00 an hour for 40 hours for 14 weeks, he is entitled to unemployment insurance for 40 weeks at $120.00 per week, for a total of $4,800.00 without working. In addition, he may also earn, through additional part-time labor, up to 25 percent of his unemployment insurance income without reduction of unemployment insurance benefits. The same person would not receive any assistance to further his education if he decided to return to school.

The foolishness of this system becomes clear when we compare the very limited availability of master's or doctoral degree scholarships. Their number is limited, and students are condemned to a low standard of living with the support of approximately $5,000 to $8,000 per year from a scholarship or from the support of a working spouse, all in order to achieve the knowledge essential for the benefit of our future.

> **Our present bureaucratic system has confused the equal opportunity for education with uniformity of education.**

Undoubtedly, there has to be a change, and the needs of the pursuit of knowledge in all its diversity will impose themselves. The pursuit of knowledge goes hand in hand with recognition of the importance of excellence.

> **Excellence by definition is nonegalitarian, and its opposite is mediocrity.**

The education system of the future will once again have to recognize the diversity of man and his potential, which has been neglected due to the bureaucratic power of centralized education systems. The solution to today's youth unemployment is to extend education, which can be effective only by breaking up the centralized, rigid, state-controlled system and creating a diversity of institutions controlled by local and regional citizens' groups to reflect the needs of the great diversity of man.

These changes will undoubtedly be implemented by the coming generation. Youth has always been the fountain of change, and the signs of change are almost tangible when one talks to and observes the new generation leaving the 12th and 13th grades. Most of them instinctively reject the right of society to control their freedom of choice and their increasing awareness of the potential of entrepreneurial opportunities.

At the teaching level we still find a large number of remnants of those who have been seduced by the promises of socialist controls, but the up-and-coming generation look upon them as irrelevant dinosaurs in our present time.

The Family

Like it or not, humans are couple-forming mammals evolved into a male-dominated society. The stress on the institution of the family began with women's changing role in the industrial society.

New technology created by entrepreneurial societies has relieved women of the arduous task of everyday toil to assure the sustenance of their family and has also radically changed their role within the family unit.

Among all segments of our society, women have the most vested interest in the entrepreneurial democracy. In dictatorial societies, men are oppressed, but women are both oppressed and abused.

While most socialist or Marxist societies have given lip service to the equality of women, entrepreneurial democracies made tremendous progress in liberating and equalizing women's stature. Prominent female figures such as Golda Meir and Margaret Thatcher and many thousands of others in high office are powerful examples of this.

Entrepreneurial society has greatly benefitted from the immense source of talent possessed by women who are now entering into the labor force. On the other hand, many have difficulty accepting their changing role. These new responsibilities, in addition to the responsibility for raising new generations, is essential to the continuity of our society and civilization.

Through public institutions, perverse Marxist and socialist influences try to turn this responsibility into a collective duty of the state.

Government-controlled and funded day care is just one frightening example. Entrepreneurial democracies believe that responsibility for raising families and caring for children should be vested in their parents and cannot be supplanted by state institutions.

First, we believe that only the family can imprint on the children the notion and experience of love. There is no substitute for parents' love of their children and children's love for their parents.

Second, the diversity of families and their right to this diversity is essential for the peaceful existence of our civilization.

It is sad that this diversity of man extends to some undesirable extreme to families who are unable to express love or care for their children, and this is the only instance when the state has the right to interfere. These exceptions notwithstanding, the family remains the strongest molecule of the complex chemistry of entrepreneurial democracy.

Today, the stress placed on the family unit is only temporary, brought about by our changing technology, and will be resolved through a new appreciation and acceptance of the freedom of women and of their most important role in the parenting of future generations.

Entrepreneurial democracy is now developing instruments through which the increasing number of working women are being provided maternity compensation to facilitate their temporary withdrawal from the labor force without undue financial hardships.

Chapter Eight

Economic Crisis and Unemployment

In slave societies there is always full employment.

The detractors of our society continually point out the inequities inherent in the diversity of man and try to blame every hardship beared by our citizens as being caused by our social/economic system.

We would all like to live in a world where there are no tornados, snow storms, dry spells or earthquakes. Most of us would like to live in a society without child molesters and maniac killers, and we would like to live in a world where there are no ups and downs in our economic activities.

Unfortunately, the roots of ups and downs of economic cycles can be found in the nature of the universe and in man himself. Nothing is stable and permanent in our world; as our universe is in continuous motion, so are human nature and activities.

There are a number of major forces of motion which provoke economic cycles. First, all human activities are inescapably influenced by the intangible forces of human motivation. Depression in the entrepreneurial spirit of man creates economic depressions. The herd instinct deeply rooted in our biological make-up turns this force into collective depressions.

A second force is the changing technology. The blacksmith inevitably became obsolete, as did the typewriter and as will printing presses and digital computers, just like the horse-drawn carriage of yesteryear. These changes always create dislocations and cycles of employment opportunities. These ups and downs in our activities are inescapable, regardless of our economic system. The systems differ only in terms of the protection offered to their citizens during a crisis.

Unemployment Insurance Benefits

The entrepreneurial democracies provide the most human and compassionate form of protection in comparison to all others, however inadequate it may be. The unemployment-benefits system of protection that exists in democratic society should be looked upon as an institution of which we can all be very proud.

Unfortunately, the perverse Marxist and socialist influences are slowly turning this institution into a politically oriented welfare benefit. This is rationalized with the political notion that everybody is willing to work and ready to work. The reality is that every benefit provided free will be abused in proportion to the generality of the rules by which it is distributed.

Nothing is easier than to create full employment. We should remember that in **slave societies there is always full employment.**

Once we accept the notion that the state has the duty to ensure uninterrupted employment for everyone, we inherently accept the notion that everyone has to work, and we must also accept the notion that the nature and quality of chosen work will be decided by those in authority.

Once we accept that the state has the duty, the authority and the right to allocate work to every citizen, we inherently accept the notion that it has the right to control not only the nature of the work but also the priority of the location where the work is required. This simply means that the state acquires the right to control the displacement of its citizens.

It is only the extreme capacity of wealth-creating power of entrepreneurial democracies and their respect for individual freedom that has created a system by which society provides assistance and support to those who are deprived for any reason of employment, with the right to look for and obtain work which is equal to their qualifications or what they perceive their qualifications to be, in the location where they want to work. What our unemployment-insurance system does is to provide a cushion to make those changes the most humane and least painful.

We very often hear the voices of those who ask for mandatory work laws for citizens on welfare or unemployment. A society of entrepreneurial democracies rejects these solutions and is willing to pay the price, because it values human dignity and freedom.

> **Mandatory work is slavery. Those who preach about indignities of unemployment benefits should reflect on the indignity of mandatory work, which is the only other alternative.**

It would be futile to attempt to create a society that would prevent the motion of economic forces from creating change. To direct our efforts toward diminishing the pain of change is the only achievable aim. In doing so, the entrepreneurial society proves to be, though not perfect, the most moral solution imposed on man by the nature of man.

Pockets of Poverty

Unemployment and pockets of poverty are found in social minorities — mostly in groups who for historical reasons lack the ability to adapt to the needs and priorities of the industrial society. Adaptation to those needs is in direct conflict with the customs and priorities of their everyday lives. Unfortunately, pervasive Marxist and socialist ideologies which dominated our thinking in the last century made it impossible to recognize the reasons for this lack of adaptation and consequently denied us the actions which would bring about improvements in the everyday lives of these minorities.

The Canadian example is instructive. In the two decades following World War II, over three million persons emigrated and found homes in Canada. A portion of those were Italians or Portuguese, and most of them had minimal education and lacked knowledge of English or French. In 15 or 20 years of residence, most of these foreigners prospered without any recourse to welfare. For example, of over 300,000 Italians in metropolitan Toronto, approximately 80 percent are home owners.

However, simultaneously, in many parts of Canada there remained pockets of poverty and chronic unemployment in areas populated by descendants of the early settlers of French or Anglo-Saxon origin, or indigenous native peoples, who for historical reasons were unable to adapt to the discipline required and imposed by industrial society and lacked the entrepreneurial spirit essential in these societies. These pockets of poverty shall continue to exist as long as we continue to deny the reality and the solutions imposed by reality, holding attitudes that are almost humorous, as illustrated by the following example.

Once, in the Ontario legislature, a socialist deputy strongly attacked and blamed the government because a member of a native settlement had died of pneumonia. The government was accused of the "crime" of not providing sufficient helicopters equipped with physicians to rapidly transport the patients to the hospital. Those amenities are readily available in the industrialized parts of our country.

Within a period of a few months, the same socialist deputy criticized the same government for its intention to allow industrial development of gas pipelines and paper mills in the area, which would disturb the traditional way of life of the natives—without recognizing the irony that equipped helicopters and nearby physicians would also interfere with the traditional way of life of the native people and that **to reap the benefit of advanced technology, one must pay the price of living with advanced technology.**

The Failure of Civilization

The examination of civilizations created by those of different social backgrounds in different parts of the world shows something which is worthy of attention. The low standard of living in Mexico or Nicaruaga, compared to Japan or Canada, cannot be explained by a lack of riches in natural resources, an unfavorable climate or exploitation by rich nations. The explanation is found in the level of the social development of these nations. The demagogy, which blames the low standard of living of these nations on exploitation by others, does not withstand scientific scrutiny.

> **The low standard of living of the South American nations in comparison to the North American nations is due to the social background of these nations.**

On the North American continent, the colonizers were individuals devoted to freedom and the division of powers within society. The greatest motivation for the immigrants was to further this division of power to protect their individual rights from the overwhelming power of the state.

Conversely, on the South American continent, the colonizers were representatives of the Spanish and Portuguese empires, proponents of all-encompassing totalitarian power of the state, dominated by the brutal forces of the Inquisition.

Totalitarian powers are always totally corrupt, and justice is dispensed at the whims of the holders of power. For humanity to survive, **it must develop the skill of corruption, matching its wit against these oppressive powers and look upon the institution of government not as protector, but as exploiter.**

People who have been raised and who live in these environments for generations find it difficult to adapt to a free society. They developed a natural resistance to the eradication of corruption inherited from the totalitarian state.

For states to regain the trust of the people, essential for the functioning of an entrepreneurial democracy, they have to rigorously implement the division of power with all its painful stress of change. It is a process with slow progression through education and the exposure of the people to the continuously improving administration of justice. There is another solution practiced by Marxist societies, where all social resistance is brutally eliminated by mass deportation of indigents into new environments, as in Nicaragua, Vietnam and Ethiopia, and the totalitarian imposition of the will and the values of those new societies where corruption continues to reign in the name of the righteousness of Marxist ideology.

Chapter Nine

The Politics of Fear

The forces aligned against entrepreneurial democracy play the politics of fear. Fear is their greatest coercive weapon. The fear of sickness, the fear of hunger, the fear of being powerless. Man is immune to the coercion of fear when he understands the strength of the entrepreneurial democracy and the knowledge that the only commodity in short supply on earth is freedom and the knowledge of man.

Since mankind's earliest days, fear has been used for its power of coercion to subjugate him and temper his thirst for freedom. It was the tool of the medicine man in primitive societies, who used the fear of spirits. In more recent times, it was the tool of dictators, and today, fear is the most powerful tool in the hands of the adversaries of the freedom of man.

These merchants of fear are polluting men's minds with continual prophecies of doomsday, which, according to them, can only be prevented if we abdicate our rights and submit voluntarily to rules and limitations on the exercise of our very basic rights.

Those who talk about shortages of energy, food and space on earth for all people fail to accept the reality that the only commodity in short supply on earth is **freedom and knowledge of man.**

The self-appointed new aristocrats, who try to rule by the right of their intellectual superiority perceived only by themselves, continue to predict the continuing shortages like a broken record, with the shrill voice of ancient gramophones.

Shortage of Food

They are preaching the coming shortage of food and are advocating controls in the use of land and its ownership.

The fact that entrepreneurial democracies have proven their capacity to produce not only sufficient food, but an abundance and surplus of it, has had no effect on their dogma. One of the most difficult problems entrepreneurial democracies have is coping with the ever-increasing supply of food beyond their own needs. The excess of food produced by the European Community and by the United States, in spite of the millions of acres held in fallow, is meaningless to them. The apostles of fear have no use for evidence that is contrary to their doctrines.

The reality of science, which has removed all mystery of the natural composition of the soil and brought about the production of food in soilless conditions, never reaches through the walls of their ivory towers.

The existence of the thriving Israeli agriculture, where the technology of drip irrigation has become the reality of everyday life, the evidence that by the application of technology, the amount of water needed to grow food can be reduced by 70 percent to 80 percent, with an increase in yield of up to 100 percent, is meaningless for the apostles of fear. They don't recognize the greening and blooming of the orchards and cotton fields, which produce an abundance of crops in supposedly unsuitable agricultural-production areas. The evidence of man's creativity in a free society never breaks through their fearful minds.

There is overwhelming evidence that man doesn't need rules to limit his reproductive instincts. He has proven his capacity to voluntarily take advantage of advanced knowledge and technology to reduce reproduction and allow life to continue in the most comfortable and secure way. It has been proven, with the examples of democratic nations from Italy to Japan, that once material security and spiritual freedom are achieved via the institution of democratic society, population growth has been maintained at a manageable level. The existing technology available to man permits population control in a safe and convenient manner, based on individual desires, **with no need for government intervention or regulation.**

Shortage of Water

They talk about the shortage of water when the largest part of the earth's surface is covered in water and science is not only on the threshold of an inexpensive and easy distillation process for sea water, but, in addition, is steadily increasing its knowledge of a cell-selection process which will enable plants to thrive on irrigated sea water.

The Shortage of Energy

Nothing on earth is more abundant than energy —which surrounds every iota of our existence. The sun, stars and everything on which we stand have the potential to serve our energy needs. What is in short supply is not the potential for energy but **the knowledge of the methods to harness it for use.** The major obstacle to the discovery of and knowledge about any potential new energy supply is the existence of an abundant and cheap source of hydrocarbons. Our most recent experience is very revealing.

> **The artificial shortage of supply was created by political forces hostile to entrepreneurial democracies.**

During this artificial shortage, there was an explosion of new knowledge and technology in new sources of energy and in more efficient use of the existing source. This drive toward new sources and knowledge was then cut off by the hostile political forces, who realized the self-defeating consequences of their actions. They reduced their artificial hold and the artificially high prices of their product, and maintained a surplus supply just big enough to discourage any further investment in new energy sources. The existence of an abundance of cheap hydrocarbons is hanging, like Damocles' sword, over the entrepreneurial drive for a substitute energy.

**As with food supplies, the problem is not a
shortage, but an abundance, which is the
greatest obstacle to furthering our
knowledge.**

The prophets of doom continually base their estimates on
the past and present knowledge of man, but lack the vision,
the foresight and the inventiveness of entrepreneurial man
to expand his knowledge in relation to his needs.

The powerful forces of this new aristocracy threaten
mankind with new restrictive rules and regulations in the
name of survival. Their view is a self-fulfilling prophecy, as
shown by the shortage of food and of some of the very basic
essentials of life in the Marxist societies, where they succeeded in imposing their will through rules and regulations
imposed on the unfortunate persons living in those nations.

The greatest threat to the survival and progress of mankind
is not its incapacity to create all the essentials of survival,
nor earth's incapacity to produce the environment necessary
for life, but the forces of dictatorial powers and the limitation of man's freedom to take care of his own needs.

Editorials have asked for government rules and regulations
in the use of arable land in Canada, otherwise predicting
cruel shortages in our potential food supplies. This has been
done unabashedly and without a sense of humor.

The prime example of how regulatory forces create shortages in a self-fulfilling prophecy was illustrated in a recent Canadian story appearing in a prominent Canadian newspaper.

For example, a headline in the business section of the October 24th, 1984 issue of the Toronto Star read: "Officials Fear Small Turkey, Chicken, Egg, Milk Shortages," and went on to say:

> *Shortages of small turkeys, chickens and eggs seem to be developing, according to federal government officials. On top of that, milk supplies in Ontario are tight, forcing some industrial milk processors to shut plants temporarily.*

> *The tight supplies are all occurring in products that are under supply management—in other words, production levels are set by federal marketing agencies.*

> *This year, many of the agencies have held production too low, and the result is likely to be shortages of some products, or sharply increased imports from the United States.*

The article continues:

> *Chicken imports have soared to unprecedented levels because of a skyrocketing demand for chicken fingers and nuggets. Canada has had to import 15.4 million kilograms, or 33.9 million pounds more chicken in the first nine months of this year than planned for.*

> *Some companies that buy surplus eggs and use them for commercial products like ice cream, mayonnaise or egg powder, have had to shut*

down for two or three days a week this month because they can't get enough eggs. More than nine million eggs have been imported from the U.S. this fall to meet the demand.

This is happening at a time when our all-knowing government agencies are using the iron hand of law to limit our farmers' potential to produce abundance. We are saved from shortages primarily by the surplus available from the United States. However, we should not fear. We can be certain that this example will not shake those nameless editorialists who continually call for other rules and regulations. They will simply say that there is nothing wrong with regulation, it is just a mistake of the regulators; and so we will find the answer given for 50 years now by the Soviet leadership.

In the same issue another headline reads:

"Soviets plan huge irrigation project after crop failure."

From this article we learn the following:

Chernenko, 73, acknowledged that a "substantial shortfall" was expected in the grain harvest this year, blaming the decline mainly on drought and other harmful weather conditions. It is the sixth time the grain harvest has fallen below projections. But, in unusually candid language, Chernenko also added "Agricultural production still lags behind the country's growing requirements. Despite all the achieved positive results, the problem of providing the population of many cities with foodstuffs, above all meat, is still acute." Western experts have forecast a grain harvest of less than 170 million tonnes, far below the Soviet planned production of 240.

It says it all. There is nothing wrong with the system, there is nothing wrong with the regulations; the problem is bad weather and human error. When one listens to Marxists or parlor socialists, one hears that all shortcomings of their systems are due to human error or bad weather. Like generals, they are never wrong, they just have bad luck.

On the other hand, shortcomings of entrepreneurial democracies are always due to the unworthiness of our democratic social system itself. But we can learn more by reading daily newspapers.

Another headline in the same issue states: "Oil cartel's bid to bolster price doomed to fail economists say." The article goes on to say:

> *The latest strategy of the Organization of Petroleum Exporting Countries to temporarily slash oil production by up to 20 percent in order to avert a price war is doomed to failure, prominent energy economists say.*

We can further read that the cartel proposes a 20 percent cut-back in production to create an artificial shortage and to maintain its price of $20.00 per barrel. One should remember that this oil has been profitably produced for less than $3.00 per barrel by the multinational oil companies which produced the know-how and the capital for the discovery and technology development of this energy source.

The lesson is inescapable. **Shortages are created by regulatory forces; abundance is created by entrepreneurial pursuits in an environment of freedom.**

There are advocates of the limiting of man's inquiry into and pursuit of knowledge of our universe. These advocates preach that knowledge by itself and the pursuit of knowledge beyond a certain limit will destroy man. But when we look at the natural history of the earth, what we see is overwhelming evidence that all forms of life can be eliminated or exterminated by forces beyond man's control. The only possible analytical conclusion based on history is that **the only force which can extend and prolong man's existence on earth is knowledge and the relentless pursuit of knowledge.** In an entrepreneurial democracy, the drive of the entrepreneurial spirit ensures the relentless pursuit of knowledge, and, more importantly, ensures that entrepreneurial science is applied in the fastest possible way for the betterment of man and the extension of life.

The division of the political power and the setting of limits over the entrepreneurial pursuit of knowledge and creativeness ensures a safe equilibrium between the regulatory and creative powers within the state. The extent to which both of these forces, the regulatory political powers and the entrepreneurial pursuit of knowledge, are vested in the power of the state is possibly the greatest invitation to the derailment of man's bright future.

> **The advancement of science and technology always first serves the masses and not the privileged few.**

This new intellectual aristocracy believes that the state should give the people not what they want but what they need, and obviously reserves for itself the privilege to define these needs.

Though it preaches fear, it tries to obtain the citizens' support for placing the growth of technology and science under its control through the pretense of protecting the weakest members of our society, when in actuality, advancements always first serve the underprivileged. This may be illustrated by the following examples.

Our improved capacity for producing an abundance of food has made little difference for the wealthy and powerful. The abundance on their table was always assured, but it made a difference in the life of the laborers.

The invention of the internal-combustion engine made no material change in the life of the wealthy landlord, who never walked behind horses in the field, but it made a difference to the physical comfort and lives of those who today sit on tractors.

The discovery of heating oil had no material effect on the rich, who awakened each morning to a crackling fire, but benefitted the poor, who now also enjoy the benefit of central heating without back-breaking toil.

It was the university professors in their comfortable studios who invented the notion of **artificially created want to satisfy artificial needs. For them, the desire for an automatic dishwasher, a washer and a dryer were artificial. Obviously, they had servants to take care of those chores, but the machines benefitted the life of ordinary households.**

The use and marketing of powerful deodorants has been their ridicule for decades. In the solitude of their studies and their well-washed and perfumed social environment, they did not suffer from the nauseating odors emanating from working in close proximity to human bodies, but this invention made a difference for the office workers and factory laborers locked into close proximity with one another.

The advance of scientific technology consistently serves the masses of people and much less so the privileged minorities.

When one looks upon and compares the life of the ordinary people of entrepreneurial democracies to those in Marxist states, one can conclude that the leaders of the latter nations have all the amenities of the most technologically advanced nations.

The difference is that the amenities in Marxist states are restricted to the privileged classes of the new aristocracy, while in entrepreneurial democracies they are spread over a broader and broader spectrum of the population and will continue to expand as long as there is no hindrance placed upon the march of entrepreneurial society.

The evidence of this is that in every entrepreneurial democracy, as prosperity spreads, the indigenous population refuses to do the most unpleasant or menial tasks. By necessity, these nations become importers of labor —in France it is the North Africans, in Germany it is the Yugoslavs and Turks, in the United States it is the Mexicans and Puerto Ricans and in Hong Kong it is the people of Bangladesh and mainland China.

This selective choice of work by the indigenous people and the flow of immigrants into democratic nations should speak for itself, particularly when contrasted with the mine fields and barbed wire surrounding the Marxist states to prevent the escape of their labor force.

Chapter Ten

Alternatives to Entrepreneurial Democracies

The concepts of this book are based on empirical fact. The alternatives to entrepreneurial democracy are there for all to see. We need not experiment. They are there to be observed and studied.

The Anatomy of the Soviet Union

The greatest danger to man's survival today is not the number of nuclear arms, but the expansionist and imperialist nature and spirit of the Russian empire. Understanding the Soviet Union's actions and policies is particularly weak among the entrepreneurial democracies.

On reflection, this is understandable. For people who are born into a free society, with its continual betterment of the life of the individual, where conflicts are resolved by a more or less acceptable compromise, where people are raised and live in the compassionate spirit motivated by humanistic values of Judeo-Christian teaching, it is hard, and maybe impossible, to understand the thought processes and actions of people who have lived for generations in a society ruled by despotic individuals or small minority groups. This is particularly sad because, once we understand the anatomy of the Soviet Union, its action in any given situation is predictable with almost mechanical exactness.

The Union of Soviet Socialist Republics really means the Russian Imperial State. It is the only remaining imperialist state, and should be referred to as "Russia" because the Marxist revolution in no way altered or modified its imperialistic nature, as the state created by the French Revolution did not differ from the French Imperial state of the 16th and 17th centuries as far as the object and implementation of its foreign policy and interest were concerned. In both cases, the revolution redistributed the power structure inside the state, but the objectives and interests of the state remained constant.

The great strength of the Russian state is that it rules unabashedly, knowing that it represents a small minority, and draws its moral strength from exercising its power by quasi-religious Marxist conviction. Whenever dealing with the Russian Empire, one should remember that Marxism is a reactionary force in today's world. With the fundamentalist Muslim powers they represent the two dominant reactionary forces in the evolution of mankind.

This is easy to understand when we know that no democratic nation ever voluntarily chooses communism. The communist Marxist regime always follows an autocratic regime; from Cuba to Poland, Czechoslovakia to Hungary, the communist regime has been imposed — and could only possibly be imposed — because all the vestiges of freedom of these people were destroyed and exhausted by the brutal oppression of the totalitarian regime.

The Russian Empire looks upon democracies as the greatest and most formidable obstacle to its design for world domination. It has repeatedly chosen and will always choose alliance with nationalist reactionary forces to weaken the resolve of democracy.

The Western, liberal world fails to understand that the monarchy of Iran was destroyed by a Moscow-supported alliance of the Marxist-Leninist and fundamentalist Muslim movements not because it was a reactionary force, but because it had started to evolve toward a representative democracy. Because of this, Iran became the most prominent target of the Russian Empire.

The fundamental policy of the Russian Empire is to support extremism on every political and nationally contentious issue. From Ireland to Africa, through the extensive use of the secret service, it encourages and widens divisions, thereby making impossible the peaceful settlement of contentious issues. Any political system which rules with the consent and support of its people is anathema to the interests of the Russian Empire.

The brute strength of Russian foreign policy is always first directed against democractic forces rather than against its reactionary antagonists. The only exception to this rule is when Moscow directs communist organizations to join moderate socialist forces on a temporary basis. It does this only when it perceives the possibility of becoming the dominant and ruling component within the coalition. As the possibility of taking power within a short period of time lessens, it will leave the coalition and use all its force for obstruction of the same. We have seen this evolution in Portugal, where Moscow failed, and in Nicaragua, where Moscow succeeded.

When we examine the anatomy of any imperialist state, we find that the dominant ingredient in its power is coercion. This was true in Rome, Spain, England, France and the United States. It was via the force of this coercion that states expanded their sphere of influence and preserved their imperialistic interests. The main difference between the present Russian Empire and most imperialistic states is that those states had substantial support within their own geographic boundaries and coercion only needed to be expressed visibly outside those boundaries.

The Bolsheviks came to power by relying on a very limited minority to exercise the power, which is unabashedly expressed as the dictatorship of the proletariat. By the proletariat is meant a very limited group of individuals who have appointed themselves the proletariat, so that coercion has to be used quite visibly even within Russia's own boundaries. After 70 years of brutal physical and spiritual dictatorship, the Russian state has up until today exercised its power of coercion not only over its oppressed nationalities but over the Russian people themselves. This is because of its inability to share the benefit of power with a large part of its population.

Since coercion is one of the most important ingredients of the Russian imperialist system, it is essential that we understand the workings of coercion:

coercion is effective only when it is absolute;

coercion loses effectiveness when it is totally destructive.

The preservation of the species is the most dominant force governing the life of every living thing, including man, animals and plants. There are certain individuals who are able to overcome this biological restriction, but they are the exception.

Man has an instinctive love for freedom, but this will always be overridden by his fear of extinction when coercive forces are used to subjugate freedom. Man will fight for his right as long as there is hope, or a perceived hope, of victory or survival. Some individuals will choose death versus servitude, but **man collectively will always choose to live, no matter how miserably, as long as there is hope for survival.** The only exception is when a group of men collectively perceives the inevitability of death and the choice is not really between life in slavery or death, but between death in honor or disgrace. This is true, without exception, for all races, creeds and tribes. We have been able to observe the vivid example of these forces in the terrible events of World War II. Members of the Japanese Imperial Armed Forces treated their prisoners of war with utmost brutality or disdain. Their action expressed the thought: "These men were willing to give up their arms to save their lives. They are such low creatures that they do not deserve to live." But when faced with the total destruction and certainty of death represented by the atom bomb, the same Japanese chose to live, bowing their heads to the boots of McArthur's army.

When the Russian army walked through Germany, the same men who had looked with utmost disgust upon the victims of Nazi terror dying without resistance in the death camps stood by and turned their heads when their wives and daughters were brutalized and raped by members of the Russian army. They turned their heads and chose to live. The Nazis were always careful to maintain an illusion of hope in their victims right up to the moment of death.

If we understand these forces of coercion, we can understand why the Helsinki Agreement has never been worth the value of the paper on which it was written. We can understand why every individual becomes so important to the immense Russian state, which has recognized that it rules through coercion and that this coercion can only be effective if it is absolute. Russia's actions are no different from those of plantation owners who devoted force and money far beyond the value of escaping slaves for their recapture.

Another dominant force of everyday life within the Russian empire is collective guilt. To understand this, we have to look back to the period of Stalin's rule. Stalin devised a very ingenious and cruelly simple means to maintain the power of his despotic rule: a planned and organized terror campaign against every significant and similar-thinking group of the Russian population. The well-planned elimination of thousands of innocent Russians passed through the strata of the Russian people, including the armed forces, professional groups, aristocrats, farmers and industrial groups. The cruelties and crimes perpetrated during this period were no less brutal in magnitude than those committed by the Nazis.

The diabolic ingenuity of this apparently indiscriminate, but in fact discriminating, terror completely eliminated any consideration of resistance. When the most ardent supporters of the regime are arrested and accused —when members of the secret service are killed and thrown into the same holes as their victims, when terror maintains its merry-go-round, all possible consolidation of resistance becomes impossible.

There were millions of ordinary policemen, party officials, prison guards and directors of enterprise who innocently and unwillingly played a part in executing the terror, and by the association of guilt they formed a solid wall of resistance to any change which would make the moment of reckoning possible. We saw this happening in Czechoslovakia when the socialist revolutionaries started to question the action of the secret service. It was time for drastic oppression, which became inevitable and predictable when the population started to ask for an accounting of the injustices committed against party members during the Stalinist regime. The consolidation of forces against Khruschev's rule became inevitable when he started to unveil historical secrets of the past decades. He was years ahead of his time.

As long as the generation of those associated with the guilt are still alive, they continue to represent the greatest obstacle of any evolution toward a more human and popularly supported regime within the Russian empire.

We are entering the most critical phase of our relations with Russia. The economic achievements of entrepreneurial democracies in the 1960s and 1970s have, beyond expectations, improved material wealth for their populations. This prosperity and individual freedom create an insupportable pressure on the Russian ruling class, whose failure to provide improved standards of living for its people is questioned by a larger and larger group of its own population. The unexpected prosperity and strength of the entrepreneurial democracies has been identified by the Russian Empire as the greatest danger to its stability. It was and is the cornerstone of Soviet foreign policy to arrest this material progress.

The prime objective of the Soviet Union's everyday policy is to achieve control over its bordering Western democratic nations. To achieve this objective of a subservient Western Europe, the Soviet Union relentlessly exercises its power of coercion. The build-up of armed forces stationed on the border of Eastern Europe has never been intended to be used for invasion, but strictly for coercion. There is no possible benefit to a battle which would destroy Western Europe and leave its industrial infrastructure in ruins. Western Europe has maintained its political and economic integrity only because of the assistance of the United States, the only power with sufficient strength to resist this coercion. As a consequence of this, the isolation of the United States became a requirement, manifested in the "Yankee Go Home" campaign.

Fortunately, the United States has evolved to the point where the spread of its civilization can find an outlet of expression in a spiritual form. The spiritual expansion of the American imperialism is the expression of the belief that individual freedom and the **improvement of the material well-being of individuals is possible for anyone in the world.** In practice, this manifests itself in blue jeans, McDonald's hamburgers and Coca Cola, expertise on production and distribution and the abundance of its food supplies.

The ascendance of Gorbachev to power and the changes occurring in Russia to date do not change the fundamental reasons for its adversary position. In order to understand Gorbachev, one has to give importance not to the changes, but to all that remains intact. What remains intact are the elaborate instruments of coercion and the power base through which any powerful leader can redirect the state's affairs.

Without a meaningful division of power, the liberties given today can be rapidly suppressed tomorrow. It is only a cosmetic gesture to posthumously rehabilitate innocent victims without giving the smallest thought to calling to account those who perpetrated and collaborated in the conviction of those victims. And the significance is that today's powers do not want to antagonize the instruments of oppression.

The reasons for Gorbachev's ascendance to power are noteworthy. It obviously occurred because of the failures of the previous administration in fields such as diplomacy, the military and the economy.

In **diplomacy,** the Soviet Union has found itself more and more isolated. **Militarily,** its objectives in the Near East have been defeated repeatedly by Israel and it finds itself tied down in costly wars in Africa, the Far East and South

America. **Economically**, the Soviet bloc is slowly sinking to the stature of an undeveloped country.

One can only respect the adroitness with which Gorbachev's regime tries to overcome the weaknesses it inherited, without sacrificing any of its principal tenets.

Diplomatically, the Soviet Union has been partly successful in overcoming its isolation.

Militarily, it is pushing for disengagement of conflicts without giving up the positions it has acheived thereby.

Economically, it successfully taps into the wealth of entrepreneurial democracies through direct loans and joint ventures with entrepreneurial entities of the free societies.

As the Gorbachev regime consolidates its position, it will face the realization that the measures taken internally or externally are not sufficient to meet its objectives. The Gorbachev regime will inherit the bitter fruits of the Soviet secret service's consistent support of the extremist element in every Muslim country that sought to overthrow the institution of monarchy.

At the time when entrepreneurial democracies used their influence to guide these absolute monarchies toward a broader-based division of power and toward progress through parliamentary monarchies, the Soviet Union used all its power to substitute the power of absolute monarchies by absolute dictatorship of a Marxist/Leninist—Muslim nationalist blend.

The destruction of Israel as a democratic nation was, for thirty years, and still is, the cornerstone of the Soviet foreign policy. It is the Soviet Union's imperial objective to establish a secular Palestinian state subservient of its national interest. The very nature of Marxist/Leninist tenets make the conflict with Judaism inevitable. Israel's geographic position only makes this hostility more violent and urgent.

During the Gorbachev regime's adroit direction, the objective remains constant, but the means to achieve it has been shifted from direct military confrontation to well organized destabilization of Israel and to successfully focus the liberal conscience toward the hardships of the homeless Palestinians.

The history and consequences of this disastrous policy are still being written. Undoubtedly, it has all the potential to bring on a world crisis not dissimilar to the emergence of German national socialism in the 1930s.

In the coming years, the Soviet Union will face the realization that changing its method of diplomacy is not sufficient. It will have to change its objectives and re-evaluate its national interest.

Advanced technology demands an absolute division of power and instant decision-making capacity which is in direct conflict with the centralized powers of its Marxist regime. Without the division of power, it is impossible to achieve the efficient and productive economic system inherent in advanced technology.

The economic and political pressures sooner or later will force Russia to reconsider its national priority as has happened in all other imperialist states.

Clearly, the future of mankind will depend on the ability of the entrepreneurial democracies to help bring about a change in the Russian Empire's imperialist spirit. This is an attainable objective when it is disassociated from any notions of changing the nature of the present social and economic system.

Conclusion

If the security of shelter, food and medical care is freedom, then the animals in the zoo are the freest ones of all.

Freedom is not an abstract notion, as some would like us to believe. Freedom is simply an opportunity to make choices, and the acceptance of the consequences of one's choice.

Any social system that attempts to protect its citizens from the consequence of their choices inevitably will deprive its citizens of the freedom of choice.

Entrepreneurial democracy recognizes that there is no absolutely equal opportunity for choice. There are limitations inherent in the diversity of man. Some of us are born handicapped, physically or mentally; some of us are handicapped by family environment, from not being motivated to reach our full potential.

It is the fundamental tenet of entrepreneurial democracies to secure the basic needs of all of their citizens, but to reject the notion of depriving the productive segments of its citizens from the benefit of the wealth gained through a productive wealth-creating life.

Entrepreneurial democracy's morality is directed by religious and humanistic values and not by socialist terror.

When we examine the origin of wealth of the most privileged segment of entrepreneurial societies, we find that there are some who arrived at their favorable position by abusing the freedom secured by democracy and by using their wealth to the detriment rather than to the benefit of society.

Conversely, when we closely examine the backgound of the most deprived segment of our citizens, we will find that some of them are evil, uncaring individuals who have gone through life exploiting, like blood-sucking parasites, the generosity, the freedom and the compassion of our society.

Entrepreneurial democracies recognize man's limitation to administer absolute justice based on individual merits. We accept the imperfection of our system, but we create the perfect equilibrium of a stable society continuously in motion toward better justice for all.

Entrepreneurial people in an environment of freedom are bringing about knowledge and changes in our technology which offer unlimited potential for prosperity and abundance to all.

New technology holds the promise of extending man's dominion over our solar system. All of these potentials can be realized only in a world guided by a cooperative spirit in an environment of freedom and respect for the diversity of individuals. In the new world there is no room for absolute power, guided by religious, racial or ideological superiority.

Entrepreneurial democracies represent the hope of a social system to extend man's life through time.

As we enter into the last decade of the 20th Century, we are witnessing the sad results of the imposition of the Marxism-socialism on some of the world's subjugated nations.

We would like to hope that the coming generations will be spared the heartaches and deprivation imposed on nations by the fanatics of utopian ideologies.

Unfortunately, citizens of the entrepreneurial democracies will have to continue to carry the burden to protect their freedom in the pursuit of the betterment of life for all mankind.

The battle between the passive and active, between the regulators and the creators is a neverending struggle. No sooner do we witness the proof that entrepreneurial men refuse to live in accordance with the Marxist-socialist textbooks than mankind is faced with the emergence of the environmental prophets, this time waving the green flag.

While entrepreneurial man devotes his talent and knowledge to improving the environment by reducing and eliminating the harmful effects of technology, these new prophets are preaching that the only road to survivial is the redistribution of existing resources, and condemn the creation of additional new wealth. We should not be surprised. We can be certain that when the first entrepreneurial man put a plow onto the land, there was vehement opposition from many. And so it shall be forever and ever.

We can also be certain that humanity will refuse to live according to the textbooks of these new prophets, so they will try to impose their will by the rules and regulations and dictatorial powers on uncooperative humanity.

As with all other reactionary forces of yesteryears, they will face the reality that there will always be men with the spirit of freedom in their heart and thirst for knowledge in their minds, and mankind refuses to live in an orderly zoo...and detests the zookeeper.